Goodbye Clartie

HENRY BREWIS

FARMING PRESS

First published 1994

ISBN 0–85236–290–0

A Catalogue Record for this book is available from the British Library

Published by:
Farming Press Books, Wharfedale Road
Ipswich IP1 4LG, United Kingdom

North American Distributor:
Diamond Farm Enterprises, Box 537
Alexandria Bay, NY 13607

Typeset by Winsor Clarke Typesetting, Ipswich
Printed and bound in Great Britain by
Redwood Books, Trowbridge, Wiltshire

Early Warning...

The traditional British peasant may already be an endangered species.

Sightings of the genuine beast are becoming increasingly rare ... anxious anthropologists fear the animal could well become extinct, even before the EEC goes bust, or Jacques Delors becomes Pope.

With the threatened demise of this remarkable creature a unique way of life will disappear altogether — a peculiar (bloody-minded) behavioural pattern will vanish — and rural Britain no longer echo to the lyrical mutterings of auld-fashioned farming folk.

True, several small noisy groups can still be observed clinging desperately to the railings at a mart somewhere. As you drive through the countryside en-route to a designated picnic area or Safari theme park, you may yet see some poor half-crazed soul waving his IACS form, dancing blindly through his set-aside.... And yes, you can occasionally still hear the pathetic cry of a bandy-legged shepherd, as he encourages his useless dog to round up the ewe quota.

But their time is running out.... The bureaucratic Gobbledygook Patrols are everywhere, determined to cover the land with a million new rules and regulations. The poor bewildered peasant is almost submerged under a mountain of paper.

Perhaps already some excited green-tinted townies and the new army of power-crazed officials imagine the countryside is at last theirs ... by divine right, or some obscure Common Market dictate....

Bollocks! Not yet ... it still belongs to the peasant ... but only just, mind ... only just ... and there's barely a handful of them left.

'... no, I don't know how these things work either, pet, — but just fax m' supper over in about half an hour, will y' ...?

'Doesn't matter what system we use ... I'm afraid you're still knackered!'

Find the Peasant...

The genuine peasant comes in all shapes and sizes ... long ones, short ones, loved ones, rotten ones — but there are half a dozen things they all have in common....

1) Hands and feet that appear to belong to someone else....

2) A perma-tan from the second button on his shirt to the cap line on his brow ... and from just above the elbow down to his (damaged) thumb nail. The rest of his body is 'off-white' — having never been exposed....

3) Because of the unpredictable nature of the job, he will keep his trousers secured with braces, belt, and a length of baler twine....

4) He will use a distinctive rural vocabulary which, especially on bad days, no townie person will understand. All things considered, this is good news....

5) He can display a moving concern for the well-being and comfort of dumb animals — which will change dramatically if the stupid little sod won't suck....

and 6) He suffers from a peculiar farming disorder known as selective amnesia, which allows him to forget the last lambing, and begin the next with blind, irrational confidence....

The simple townie out for a drive in the country may encounter the occasional imposter of course ... a man who claims to be of peasant stock, yet who fails to meet the above criteria. These deceivers are quite easily recognisable, however. They may well be wearing what passes for the accepted rural apparel — wellies, green overalls, tweed cap, shepherd's crook and so on. But look closely, all this stuff is almost brand new, without blemish, spotlessly clean ... and not a hint of that unmistakable farmyard fragrance which clings to the traditional peasant, such as rotten sheep's feet, pig slurry, or silage effluent. No, these boys are not for real, and have probably just inherited half of Hampshire and a Mitsubishi Shogun from their twice-widowed granny ... or (a more recent phenomenon this), they are successful townie lawyers who, having defended a few wayward MPs in the high court, can now easily afford to purchase a farm, a yacht, Scotland, or whatever....

The genuine peasant is not 'a dedicated follower of fashion' ... and will happily wear his own peculiar 'designer gear' until it's able to stand up unaided ... and Gladys is forced to replace it with something washed but identical.

That hard-wearing suit he was persuaded to buy for cousin Hilda's wedding in '52 will of course do nicely for all the other nuptials and funerals. When it eventually displays serious signs of fatigue, it becomes part of the mart ensemble (but only if the pockets are still intact). Ultimately, by now a shadow of its former self, it will be relegated to the working wardrobe ... a motley collection, usually worn under a smelly all-purpose overall which covers any embarrassments which might be smouldering beneath....

Sep's view of feminine fashion may appear to be a bit cagey.... He might even seem hesitant to discuss the subject, but don't imagine for a moment he's entirely disinterested.... The fleeting glimpse of shapely thigh or a plunging neckline might hardly be enough to get his mind off the lambing ... but it has been known to disturb the man on a warm night!

'... Dad, believe me ... she just wouldn't let him suck!'

10

'... well y' always thought they were common anyway, didn't y' ?'

'Well of course I've given them up, pet ... but you wouldn't begrudge this poor dying' yow
her last puff, would y' ?'

'You've got that dog spoilt ...'

The Wife...

The wife of the traditional peasant is considered extremely fortunate to have 'acquired' such a charming, sensitive partner (at least by the charming, sensitive partner she is). Just how she got so lucky has always been a bit of a mystery ... what on earth attracted her to the bloke in the first place? Was it his enchanting manners ... his sophisticated dress sense ... his bewitching conversation — or just the prospect of an idyllic life together devoted to slavering lambs, slug-infested wheat and calves with diarrhoea?

The truth probably is that both parties considered matrimony to be a reasonably good idea at the time. The time being about 3.30 am after the Annual YFC Dance.

...And Kids...

Once upon a time the embryo peasant was largely unaware that any other worthwhile profession existed. Education was an irritating intrusion into a career already developing nicely by the time he was two and a half.

Encouraged by a father who considered it a family tragedy if his son was tempted into accountancy, banking or (God forbid) the civil service, the lad was quickly initiated into the mysteries of farming.

Mother might have secretly hoped for something a little more rewarding, something artistic perhaps ... particularly if she'd already observed the rapid metamorphosis of her husband (and probably her Dad as well) from cuddly, athletic superman, to bad-tempered, arthritic chauvinist.

Daughters have been increasingly wary of peasant suitors for some time now, perhaps reluctant to commit themselves to a partner who may be emotionally involved with someone called Sweep!

'Stop sulking ... he'll help you with your IACS form when he's finished his homework ...'

'Look, I've invented the wheel ... It could revolutionise the treatment of lame yowes!'

'... I think that'll have t' do, pet ... I'm sure we've exceeded the quota already!'

'... drugs, sex, violence, death.... I mean what chance have we got when we grow up?'

'Believe me, pet ... if we're not all tagged, documented and recorded, we probably won't qualify for the pension!'

The Farm...

Urban readers should be aware that the land on which the peasant lives and works, no matter how barren, clarty or stoney, is (to him) the most important piece of territory in the whole universe. Far more valuable than Yorkshire or the Sheikdom of Kuwait (unless of course you actually make him a firm offer)....

Clartiehole Farm is home (be it ever so draughty), business (be it non-profit-making) and above all a refuge from the 'outside world'.

That's another place where mad women chop off male dangly bits ... where pregnant Wrens claim half a million compensation for the growing inconvenience ... where burglars are released on bail so they can make a better job of it next time. Where people sue each other for harassment, and politicians blather.

If you think this smells of a sectarian 'them and us' attitude, 'rural v urban' — you're absolutely right. The peasant views the city as a dump, where parents are invariably single, kids are out of control, and life on social security is the norm. He believes the reintroduction of the death penalty and syrup of figs would cure most problems.

But back to the farm.... Any un-enlightened townies who imagine they can just troll out to Clartiehole with all their fat relations and picnic in a field of barley, should pause to consider how they might react if Sep and his entourage arrived unannounced for a little alfresco nosh in the front garden of 25 Acacia Avenue ... complete with football, ghetto blaster, crate of lager, and a pair of crapping collies!

Don't worry ... it's not very likely ... he'd never find your place. Once off his own midden, he's lost.

Trespassers...

Whether he likes it or not, the beleaguered peasant is forced to accept that growing townie hordes will inevitably creep out from the dark, polluted city. And you might ask, 'well who in their right mind can blame them?'

Well the peasant can, and undoubtedly *will* if they don't behave themselves ... or if he's in a bad fettle anyway ... or if it's raining ... or not raining ... or if he had a dead yow that morning ... or if next door's finished his harvest already....

Indeed all strangers to his 'kingdom' may be viewed, initially at least, as potential terrorists. Even other country folk are often barely tolerated some days.

But of course a neighbour will inevitably call to borrow a tractor, or retrieve his own muck-spreader. Perhaps he's come to see if Sep's lambs are scoured t'death like his ... maybe he's heard a rumour that Gladys has buggered off with the bin-men.... More likely, it's a lousy wet morning and he just wants to compare a few random disasters over a cup of coffee ... and that's always acceptable — provided his disasters are much worse than yours!

Others who violate his air-space may *not* get a cup of coffee. A posse of jabbering ramblers for instance — resplendent in woolly socks, multi-coloured anoraks, a jangling concerto of aluminium cooking pots, and Wainwright's Guide to Anglo-Saxon Burial Sites, who come striding through the farmyard just as our hero is kicked in the groin by a disturbed Charolais calf.

Even the most persistent salesmen, superbly trained at countless seminars to disregard everything from protestations of insolvency to simply unhinged abuse, soon learn to stay inside their company Cavalier, with the engine running, and the window open no more than a couple of inches.

21

'I expect he's hidden away somewhere, counting all his subsidies ...'

'... now then, Constable, what have we here ... Little Bo Peep in a spot o' bother perhaps?'

'I'm pretty sure *he* wasn't marked on the map!'

'Remember that farmer who was upset just because we had a picnic in his cornfield?
… well it's him!'

'I fear we might be in a spot of bother here, Sir ...'

'... you'll let us know if we're in the way, won't you?'

Officialdom-de-dom...

To the dismay of Sep & Co., the traditional intruder has now been supplemented by a far more virulent strain — a whole new army of 'bureaucratic busybodies'. They fly in like avenging aphids to settle on livestock numbers and badger setts.... They monitor cereal acreages, they measure hedgerows, and check woodland, footpaths, stone walls, ditches and old buildings. They wander the less favoured areas, the areas of special scientific interest and great landscape value. They seek out empty spray cans, wobbly ladders and dangerous wufflers. They issue licences, approve plans, consult on conservation, issue 'passports'.

And all the time the perplexed peasant is filling in another vast, mystifying form which usually arrives with a vast 'helpful' explanatory encyclopedia, apparently designed to confuse him even further....

But there's no escape. Somehow or other that impenetrable questionnaire has to be completed. He must be painfully polite to the official Ayatollahs ... it's essential ... it could determine whether or not the EEC sends him a fat cheque.

Sometimes he thinks it might be an easier life with no subsidies at all, and the freedom to do whatever he fancies — sink or swim. It might be tough for a while, but Gladys could always take in washin', couldn't she?

Meanwhile he must abide by the new order ... or some sneaky satellite hovering in the ionosphere will swoop down and zap his yow quota!

Europe...

Sep blames all this hassle on the Extravagant European Community ... an enormous organisation run by a plague of political gnomes primarily for the benefit of themselves — with a massive bureaucracy that feeds on the necessity to invent something new to do in order to justify its own existence and ever-expanding budget. Consequently these blathering hordes scurry about the continent from one five-star hotel to another, holding long-winded conferences on where to hold the next long-winded conference.... Occasionally they might discuss a single currency or the shape of a cucumber. They travel first class of course, and build gigantic new office blocks filled with exotic plants and secretaries.

The continental peasant appears to treat most of their output with a pinch of garlic.... He either ignores it, or cheats....

The Spanish pig is still slaughtered in the back yard, a bull is impaled in the stadium. Italian cattle are chased through the streets, cats roam the restaurant, a dog sits hopefully in the butcher's shop. Greek olive trees meander from one side of the mountain to the other, while the mafia shuffles beef about. The French set fire to imported sheep and spread muck in the Champs Elysées.... Fraud is an international sport.

Be that as it may, down at Clartiehole Farm, grumbly old Sep is beginning to realise that without the considerable influence of his objectionable continental cousins, he might've been put out to grass already....

29

'I'll take the cattle, pet ... you bring the paperwork ...'

'… not a word to anybody … but I reckon we've had 0.02 acres rent-free for the last twenty-seven years!'

'... I think everything you'll need's in there somewhere ...'

'... and we call this the Bureaucrat Room ...'

'... I blame the helpful booklet they sent.... That pushed him over the edge before he even got started!'

34

'... don't be silly ... they'll just be EEC spies checkin' on your oilseed rape acreage ...'

Educatin' Acacia Avenue...

The average townie has no real understanding of agricultural problems. He either persists with a rural fantasy filled with lovable domestic animals grazing happily in a meadow full of buttercups — or a prime-time television horror story of greedy farmers who systematically poison everything, while earning almost as much as a dentist.

It's not quite like that. Cyril from suburbia with wife and 2.4 spoiled brats, setting out for 'a run in the country' needs to be 'enlightened'....

(i) Cattle...

Contrary to a widely held belief, all bovines are not necessarily bulls or mad cows — however this doesn't mean you shouldn't be very careful at all times. For instance a suckler cow can often become quite deranged while protecting her new-born calf, and be persuaded that a carelessly parked Volvo is a serious threat. A heifer who is 'mad-a-bullin' ' (technical term for 'aroused') has been known to gallop through brick walls in a frantic search for a bit of hanky-panky.

But of course bulls are the really big, dangerous things — and on no account should townies try to feed them sweeties, or attempt a meaningful conversation.

This is why Sep is sometimes inclined to put his most cantankerous Charolais in a field which has a public footpath running through it — especially if he doesn't entirely agree with the route of the footpath.

Dairy cows are another species altogether ... but don't be fooled by their docile nature ... there is danger here as well. You won't know it, but these beasts have probably been grazing lush rye grass all day, and may suddenly react as if on a diet of vindaloo and lager.

'I think I've been quite seriously harassed, Daisy ...'

'... I don't think Joseph is entirely convinced about this ...'

'C'mon, y' wimp … they're not *that* cold!'

'... and we're very lucky today ... something you rarely see now ... a fleeting glimpse of a farmer on a bike!'

'We've got a quota for 28.4 cows ... and I suppose this one is about point four ...'

(ii) Sheep...

Having negotiated the herd of abluting Holsteins, our townie travellers will sooner or later come upon a flock of sheep. Cyril will point enthusiastically and shout, 'Look, some lambs!' Mrs Townie will say 'Aaahh,' in a soppy voice, and the brats in the back will briefly cease their whingeing, long enough to peer over the hedge at these weird creatures.

We have to assume the family know little or nothing about sheep. There may be a fragile connection with thermal underwear and mint sauce — but no proper understanding of the complex nature of the species. Consequently they will be surprised to see several lying upside down ... perhaps with a crow perched on the upturned belly. This is perfectly normal.

Others may be hobbling pitifully about the field, probably coughing.... There may be a ewe with head down, looking miserable, and yet another hurtling about, crashing into trees

and fences apparently out of (what we euphemistically refer to as) her tiny mind. There's nothing unusual about any of this. The peasant will tell you that sheep (like lemmings) are eager to self-destruct. Sheep only have *terminal* diseases ... nowt trivial. There is a well-known piece of farming lore which says, 'a sheep's worst enemy is another sheep'. Sheep have always fully understood this.

A Freudian shepherd (if there were such a thing) might suggest that this tormented existence is due entirely to the tragically inadequate sex life of the animal. Townies on a late autumnal excursion may have observed ewes with brightly coloured backsides. No, this is not a desperate peasant whim to brighten up dull November days ... this indicates the mating season for sheep is in full swing.

For many of God's creatures spring is the time for the 'sap' to rise ... but the mule yow predictably prefers cold, wet weather to copulate. For her, sex occurs but once a year, and so you might imagine she'd make the most of it. But no, t' hell with the chattin' up preamble … no time for any courtin' … no soft lights, violins or vintage wine on a balmy evening for this girl. Not a chance, just a quick one-night stand in the middle of a twenty-acre field. There's this frantic tup with a curled top lip and a bloody great crayon strapped to his chest, ricocheting about among forty bored females … and it's probably pissing down!

It's a miracle there's ever a lambing at all. There is, of course, but that story is far too horrific a tale for sensitive townie folk to contemplate … a video nasty likely to corrupt the mind of any emerging sadist in Acacia Avenue.

'Well, in spite of New Miracle Biowash, they still retain that familiar Mule yow fragrance
... don't y' think?'

'If one of the little buggers doesn't perish by tomorrow, I'll be very disappointed ...'

'... right ... I think he's probably lost count by now ...'

'… was it the Bishop of Durham who said he didn't believe in Hell? … Well quite obviously he never did a lambin'!'

'Don't look back, you fool ... they're gaining on y '!'

'Don't be ridiculous, *that* won't work ... she's been dead since Tuesday!'

(iii) Gee-Gees...

Gone are the days of massive, plodding, flatulent horses called Queenie or Prince who did everything in slow motion dressed up in bits of leather and brass.

Nowadays the only horses you'll see are part of the Hunt (which we'll come to later) or the little arrogant, pot-bellied pony belonging to the daughter of some successful couple who've emigrated from suburbia and bought the old vicarage. *They* are country people now, and daughter Amanda (or Abigail or Lucy or whoever) will inevitably want her own miniature 'Desert Orchid' with all the appropriate gear. He'll be fed on high-protein pony nuts, the best hay (in small bales) and Maltesers.

He's a lot more expensive to keep than the average labrador, but of course he's perceived as an essential part of well-heeled rural life ... like your own septic tank ... and knowing the christian name of the plumber and the postman.

Amanda could grow up to be quite a competent horsewoman ... might even join the pony club, compete at shows, follow hounds — and maybe the special relationship with D.O. will be but the first of several such 'love affairs'.

However, all parents beware ... this early passion can quickly cool in the flickering light of puberty. Almost unnoticed, like a hole in your welly ... sex creeps up and bites the poor lass. Before you know it some quite unsuitable spotty youth, doing GCSE mocks and playing percussion in a heavy metal band, has much more to offer than a smelly, spherical cob who has to be brushed and mucked out every day. Spotty, drum-beating Wayne gets all the Maltesers now, and Mummy ends up with a shovel and the wheelbarrow.

'... and I suppose you think that's very clever ...'

'... for God's sake, Mother, it's hardly the Cheltenham Gold Cup!'

'Will you please stop feeding that disgusting animal ...!'

(iv) Dogs…

The most important dog on the rural scene is still the faithful collie … certainly in the opinion of any proper peasant it is. No sloppy Lab, yappy Jack Russell or dumb Doberman can match auld Sweep for character, style and resilience — often in the face of unparalled abuse.

On rare occasions the townie tourist may be lucky enough to observe one of these remarkable creatures at work … though it should be pointed out that all collies are not in the same super-league as those seen on TV. In 'One Man and his Dog', Meg from Merthyr Tydfil responds eagerly to any shrill Welsh whistle … roars off in a great wide arc to gather sheep miles away … cleverly and gently brings them back to her boss … eases them into the little pen (almost closes the gate herself). Never a wrong word…. Magic!

Tweed from the Borders, Paddy from County Galway, Angus from Aberdeen, all do more or less the same…. Seldom is there cause for the shepherd to scream bleeped obscenities, hurl his fancy stick, or completely lose his composure and tear off up the hill in a desperate spluttering mission to 'strangle the bastard!'

Our friend Sweep, however (your everyday run o' the mill fourth division dog), might well set off with the very best of intentions, with exactly the same thoughts as the super star — only to stop twice on the way for a pee, roll in some cow muck, chase a hare into the next parish … and completely forget what the plan was in the first place.

Later, perhaps persuaded by a severe lecture, or a bloody good hidin', he might be inspired to smartly shed off a single startled gimmer … and enthusiastically remove her left lug.

Sometimes, especially if he hasn't been out and about for a day or two, Sweep can become quite excited, intoxicated by a pent-up desire to please — and on these occasions can gather the flock with such vigour that several poor auld yows may be left scattered all over the hill, upside down and breathless (I mean *totally* breathless!)

Be advised, the shepherd will not want a group of grinning townie twits leaning on the gate at such a time, especially if they're silly enough to make comments like, 'we'll give 'im five for the gather and two for the drive … he he he….'

It should also be realised that Sweep is not the spoilt, pampered domestic pet you may be familiar with in the city … nothing remotely like that perfumed poodle prancing about in Lavender Gardens, or the arrogant Afghan down Laburnum Drive. This dog is a worker, a member of staff … Clartiehole is his domain, and should he chance upon a strange townie picnic party on his patch, he will have no reservations about stealing your smoked salmon sandwiches, relieving himself on the Otterburn rug … and (as an encore) becoming romantically attached to your mother-in-law's left leg.

Sweep is disgusting … his personal hygiene non-existent. Often covered in whatever revolting substance happens to be lying about the farm, he invariably stinks to high heaven.

Sep will de-louse the hound now and then, push a worm tablet down his throat, and maybe once a year hurl him into the sheep dipper after the sheep have been through (if he can catch 'im).

Understandably Gladys is less than elated to have this wretched beast in the house. Nevertheless, a kip by the kitchen fire on a bleak day is a real bonus for the weary collie dog … his atrocious odour and surreptitious farting becoming more and more unbearable as he warms up.

But then Sep isn't much better — so she probably won't make a big fuss about it….

'I think Sweep's run away ... can't find him anywhere.... Maybe I was a bit too hard
on 'im this morning ...'

'Oh my God ... what's he been up to now?'

'Lie down, Sweep!'

'Sweep ... stop that nonsense!'

Harvest Time...

An autumnal trip into the byways will inevitably bring the townies face to face with a big yellow (or red or green) monster. It's called a combine. On a country road there is no way past a combine ... the car must reverse — to Ipswich if necessary! This is peasant country, tractor and trailer country ... big, nasty machine country ... and townies in silly Sierras could (accidentally) be swept into the dyke back.

This is harvest time ... a period of great cardiac-inducing stress (second only to lambing).

The harvesting peasant is not to be trifled with. He's spent a year and a fortune nurturing this crop to golden ripeness. He's completed the Arable Acreage forms, the set-aside declarations, beaten off pests and diseases, worried himself silly through snow, frost and floods — until now in glorious August (when everybody else is on holiday)

it's ready to cut ... get some cash back at last ... pay some bills ... all systems go! What he doesn't need is a wet week, or a shower of excitable strangers anywhere near the action!

No proper peasant ever forecasts the crop yield or the profit before he actually gets the weight tickets back ... and the cheque is in the bank. He's old enough (and almost wise enough) to know that a lady called Providence is waiting behind a tree somewhere, dressed in black, with a fiendish grin on her face ... waiting to be tempted ... ready to kick him in the wallet, and confound all his pompous predictions. Well, let's face it, combines can break down, tractors have punctures, a contractor might be kidnapped ... a hurricane can blow up from County Durham.

Gladys (who is probably hardly as old, but infinitely wiser) just gets the supper ready, fumigates his socks — and says nowt provocative till it's all over....

'So how was it for you, darling? Personally I feel the earth's still moving!'

'It was the old welly socks that did the trick.... Since the wife hung them up there hasn't been a crow or a pigeon anywhere near ...'

'Well, these randy little buggers aren't from outer space, that's for sure!'

'Get out, y' smelly old thing.... Until you've had a bath this room is a Less Favoured Area!'

'That was next door inviting us over for supper ... he must've finished his harvest!'

Urban Dreamin'…

When Sep was a lad there was a school, a post office cum grocery store, a policeman and a blacksmith in the village. Almost every house or cottage was occupied by someone involved in (or on the fringe of) agriculture.

From the 'Big House' some well-bred aristocrat surveyed his estates, chased foxes and chambermaids, and acted the enlightened Landlord, without ever getting *too* close to the 'lower orders'. Ah, those were the days….

In less than half a lifetime came the revolution, and with it the moneyed migratory townies on their relentless pursuit of the good life.

They've fought or bought their way from the two-up, two-down in Sebastopol Terrace, to the semi in Marlborough Crescent, to the detached three-bed villa in Elm Tree Road, and now on to the 'Forge' in Clartiehole Village.

For some, there's only one more rung left on the ladder to 'heaven' … a piece of land! A little five-acre plot could well be enough to constitute 'a place in the country'. Somewhere for Amanda's fat pony and the multicoloured cross country jumps six inches high. A few vintage sheep limping about in an organic wilderness of weeds might complete the picture of pastoral paradise.

For someone else *one* acre could be enough to impress friends still stuck in Wolverhampton. None of them were ever quite sure how much an acre was anyway … and only discover it's a lot if it's all lawn.

Others will acquire 'a field'. They'll buy Disney-like doe-eyed stirks, feed them 'After Eights', and talk to them all day … before selling them three years later at a loss.

All this make-believe farming doesn't matter

too much, so long as Daddy is with a firm of solicitors in the City, or Mummy likely to inherit Tescos. To the old peasant quietly chuckling behind the hedge, it only confirms what he suspected all along ... the city gent can't do Sep's job, and Sep certainly couldn't do his. The point is, Sep never wanted to....

Of course, some of his pals will have contributed to these changes in the rural scene. And who can blame them if they discover the old tumble-down byre is worth more than the rest of the farm put together.

But a word of warning. The countryside may *almost* be a peasant-free zone now — but it certainly isn't crime free....

Looking for easy pickin's, the criminals have seeped out from the city like the overflow from a bunged-up septic tank. There are three main reasons for this discharge....

1. The influx of well-heeled immigrants who can afford to convert a simple rustic abode into an executive des. res. full of pinchable objets d'art — and a couple of tempting BMWs in the drive.

2. The disappearance of the policeman from the rural beat to cruise up and down the motorway.... (All except two overweight coppers who occasionally hide behind the old Post Office in downtown Clartiehole, waiting to arrest a dastardly peasant in his pickup as he roars to the mart at 33.2 mph.)

and 3. The emergence of teenage townie tearaways in stolen Astras who've got nothing better to do than rob naive country folk. They know they're very unlikely to be caught ... or if they *are*, can plead a severely deprived inner-city childhood, parental abuse, a lesbian granny, victimisation at school, police brutality ... and walk free with a grin on their spotty faces!

'I believe you, madam … a very rare breed indeed….But unfortunately so is the peasant farmer willing to give you a bid for it …'

'What's the problem? … It's just a bloody stone wall … who's gonna object?'

'... I don't remember Clint Eastwood ever havin' this problem!'

'Nothing too over the top, Sharon … just charming, idyllic, exciting potential, mature garden
… the usual stuff will do nicely!'

The Environment...

It was always there, of course, all over the place ... wherever you looked there was 'environment'. Maybe everybody just took it for granted. Then quite suddenly people began to think about it, talk about it ... worry about it. Politicians figured there might be a few votes in it, made lots of speeches about it, passed new laws to protect it. 'It's at risk,' they said, 'it's being vandalised,' they said — 'and the peasant is largely to blame,' they said.

'What, who me?' cried Sep. 'I was just mindin' m' own business ... I never touched it ... it's that hole in the ozone layer, it's the acid rain ... it's all that industrial waste!'

'Ah yes, we know all about that,' they muttered darkly, 'but it was you who sprayed gallons of dangerous stuff all over your crops, made silage instead of hay, ploughed up old meadows, and injected your sheep with strange medicines!'

Well, isn't that what I was supposed to do?' he asked, shrugging his shoulders. 'I mean, produce more grub, help the balance of payments, be efficient ... move with the times ... eh?'

'That was yesterday, you fool,' they snarled angrily. 'Trouble is you were far too bloody clever — we don't need all this super-duper production any more.... We don't know what to do with it! Anyway, you're just polluting the rivers, threatening the poor old Barn Owl, pulling out hedgerows, turning Lincolnshire into a desert ... It simply is not environmentally friendly — slow down you greedy old git!'

'But I have to make a living,' protested Sep.... 'Wife and kids to support ... a mortgage like everybody else....'

'Oh very well,' they grumbled, 'I suppose

we'll have to give you a subsidy of some sort ... but you must promise to stop growing things....'

'OK — if you insist' said Sep. 'But how much do I get?'

'Ah well,' they smiled, 'that all depends. Meanwhile just fill in this barrowload of gobbledegook, and we'll see how it goes....'

Sep was looking at all the forms and scratching his head. 'What does it mean?' he asked ... 'is this permanent government policy?'

They were falling about. 'Are you completely mad?' they laughed. 'How the hell do we know ... Permanent government policy probably means until the money runs out ... this year, next year, some time....' But already their fleet of official Jaguars was heading

down the road to the Country Club, and a very long business lunch ... on the Euro expense account of course.

'Wottya makin' all the fuss about … you're on the wrong road anyway!'

'Hold everything! Stop that man! ... I'm willing to bet he hasn't got a
Waste Disposal Transit Licence!'

'I must say, I always thought such language was confined to Channel 4 after 9.30 p.m.'

'Now then, — didn't we get a rather threatening letter from you lot last week?
Something t' do with river pollution, was it?'

'I'll just get 'im ... I think he's putting some shelves up in the kitchen ...'

'... well, we just feel you might be letting the side down a bit, Jethro ...'

79

Extra Rural Activities...

For Sep there are no real alternatives to being a proper peasant. Neighbours may be persuaded to convert hemmels into executive homes, establish an olde coffee shoppe in the stable, open up the farm to eager urban visitors ... but the very thought of bleating townie school kids running all over the place, fills our hero with dread.

In any case Clartiehole would have to be seriously revamped to entertain the masses. It's difficult to imagine anybody would be fascinated as it is.

However let's think about it.... A few lame mule yowes could be penned up somewhere, I suppose. We might even sell ewe nuts at four times the going rate, and allow the children to feed them. The old dears would probably keel over and die at such treatment — especially if they had an audience. That could be a major attraction!

We might buy a Jersey cow from somebody ... Gladys could dress up as a buxom milkmaid and flog cream teas (we'd have to lock up Sweep of course, or he'd scoff the lot).

How about trips round the set-aside in the tractor link box at 50p a time? But wait a minute ... they'd fall out for sure, and then what about insurance, safety inspectors, hygiene? ... would we have to build a loo? I don't suppose they'd just go behind the hedge like normal folk, would they? And what happens if I (accidentally) whack some cheeky kid? Ye gods ... NSPCC, social services ... more bloody inspectors than customers. Forget it!

Bed and Breakfast perhaps? We could turn the back room into a honeymoon suite ... new duvet, new curtains, colour telly ... bottle of sparkly plonk and a bunch of daffs — with a bit o'luck they'd never come downstairs!

I suppose we *might* get some interesting people who'd really enjoy being on an ordinary farm ... but who wants a group of city folk watching your every move? Come to think of it, I bet they wouldn't be interesting at all ... probably mostly bank managers and school teachers talking about their pensions and early retirement.

It might be a better plan to pack in agriculture altogether and build another golf course. Yes, I can see it now ... The Clartiehole Golf and Country Club. We'd get Nicklaus to design it ... three hundred acres transformed into lush fairways. Very exclusive ... we could have the Peasant Open Championship ... vast tented village, television coverage. Peter Allis ... the whole works.

Some bandy-legged rural bandit could well become a household name overnight!

'... there's nothin' on the IACS form about harvestin' golf balls on set-aside!'

'... and of course all rooms have private facilities ...'

'... I'm not convinced you have the right temperament for this!'

'OK, Sweep, I think we've had enough … put them back on the bus!'

Huntin'...

The folks from Acacia Avenue will probably be totally against the Hunt ... may even perceive the 'sport', as barbaric, on a par with badger baiting and Prime Minister's Question Time. They will have highly coloured, nightmare images of the poor petrified fox hounded all over the countryside until he's torn to shreds by a pack of baying dogs. An ancient pagan ritual in which the hunters smear themselves with the blood of their victim, blow trumpets, and gallop about the landscape in fancy dress. A weird and privileged secret society that should be abolished....

Sep takes a more rational view ... he simply thinks they're all crackers! A bit like Morris dancing on horseback. In his opinion nobody in their right mind would spend a raw winter's day perched high on a demented gelding, with a wet backside and a bright blue nose.... He has little sympathy for the fox either come t'that. The scoundrel can look after himself quite nicely thank you....

So Sep tolerates this scarlet pantomime and all the 'groupies' who follow, as they view-halloo over his territory, dance sideways on the road, leave the odd gate open, frighten his geriatric yowes and upset Sweep (who has to be locked up when they're about, but still barks all day and chews the bottom of his kennel door). He suspects all hunt saboteurs are useless, skiving, unemployable 'lefties', probably on probation, and financed by some social security fiddle.... In all fairness he views some of those on horseback with only slightly more esteem ... not least because he's rather uncomfortable greeting them eyeball to kneecap as they gallop eagerly through his back yard as if hurrying to join Wellington at Waterloo!

But catch him in the right mood, and Sep is really quite happy to see the hunt ... this colourful outdoor pageant brightening up the dull winter months ... a stage for aristocratic actors, a breeding ground for thoroughbred chasers, fat Thelwellian ponies, and a pack of short-sighted hounds — especially if they're all playing on somebody else's pitch!

'Don't worry, Daphne ... once we move off they'll never keep up with us ...'

'Well, don't just sit there ... for God's sake do something!'

'CUM BYE SWEEP!!'

'... ssshhh ... you can't expect the poor creature to come out while you lot are galloping about ...'

'... so who said there was no such thing as a free lunch ... eh?'

Neighbours...

The real auld-fashioned peasant seldom falls out with any of his neighbours. You simply can't have a wild-west feud with the family next door ... even if they *are* a bunch of old farts. It may not be essential to be beer-drinking mates ... the wives don't *have* to blather endlessly on the phone like best friends ... the kids might have nothing in common at all ... but oot-bye, y' have t' get on.

Well listen ... your cows could stray onto his wheat, his cross-bred tup could ram-raid your pedigree Suffolks, you might need to borrow his wuffler, you could wake up one morning to find his bull on your lawn.... If both families didn't have a sense of proportion — somebody could end up shot!

Of course it helps greatly that the two households are not living cheek by jowl as they do in Acacia Avenue. For a start you can't hear what they're saying about you through the bedroom wall ... any private domestic disturbance is cushioned by maybe a hundred acres of grass, oilseed rape and a wood....

In Acacia Avenue, next door's dog will bark all night ... chase your cat ... ablute on your patio ... tip out your dustbins....

That pillick over the fence will put a satellite dish on the chimney ... paint his garage door bright yellow ... park his car in your gateway ... play rock music on a Sunday afternoon.... *His* tree will fall on *your* greenhouse.... He gets two thousand quid a year more than you.... They win a free Hoover holiday to Barbados ... their guests leave at three in the morning (with max revs) ... his kids each get four A levels ... his wife smiles all the time and wears very short skirts.... Quite naturally you hate the whole damn lot of them!

At least down at Clartiehole Sep can be bad-tempered and miserable in picturesque isolation, and no one's any the wiser ... no twitching curtains.

About the only time the peasant gets really upset with a neighbour is when the 'swine' finishes his harvest while Sep still has twenty acres of flat wheat to cut … and it's raining — then this cynical sod drives into the yard all smiles for a whisky. Has the man got no heart?

Actually there is one other area of possible friction … and as you might have guessed, it concerns the lady of the house….

Nothing is more likely to create domestic upheaval, or at least a period of unrelenting huff, than a bloke who is constantly taking his missus out for a bar nosh and half a carafe of rosé. This is generally considered to be above and beyond any realistic peasant obligation … too much…. Special birthdays perhaps … anniversaries maybe … end of a world war … but any more than that, and he's just showin' off — and serve 'im right if he goes bankrupt!

'Perhaps we'd better leave them alone, dear ... I think they're celebrating the end of the harvest!'

'Don't worry, we'll have a claim sorted out in no time.... The village is full of solicitors now!'

'… no, it's not hay fever … he's just allergic to government officials …'

'… listen, you lyin' toad … your cheque is definitely NOT in the post!'

The Mart...

The wandering townie should make every effort to visit a mart ... though whether he should take his missus is debatable. Ladies are not banned from livestock sales, but peasants rarely expect to see a woman at this singularly male event. Consequently, any female under seventy in an undulating sweater and displaying the merest hint of well-turned ankle, can throw the whole sale into confusion, and ruin quite a canny trade....

Furthermore, in their excitement townies tend to place themselves in a prime position at the ringside — exactly where Walter Thomson, Arthur White and Charlie Foster always stand. These fellows will undoubtedly take a very dim view if their weekly spot is occupied by a nomadic tribe of giggling strangers ... especially if they're buyin' nowt!

I mean these interlopers are obviously not eager dealers from Doncaster likely to enhance the price of 'seven-crop udders only', are they? Which brings us to the vocabulary.... It is conceivable the townie will not understand a single word the auctioneer or anybody else will utter during their entire visit. Greetings from any of the assembled peasants will at best be confined to a brief suspicious appraisal, coupled with a neolithic grunt as he passes by ... reminiscent of something you once heard on a David Attenborough programme.... And that's if he's in a good fettle....

You may overhear snippets of conversation in the ring, by the pens, in the canteen ... but they won't make much sense, punctuated as they are by strange place names, incomprehensible local expressions, and agricultural expletives. For example:

'Did y' see them skemmie bullocks off High Shield Rig? ... hellova price....'
'Moderate sorts aaltigether ... nea arse on

them, man....'
'Badly bred little buggers ... Black Mare Bog bowt them ... I think one had a stone....'
'He'll not can gi' them away i' the back end....'
'Y' got some canny sorts yersell, though....'
'Aye, I think they'll shift aalright....'
'They'll not hev been abused likely....'
'No, runnin' thick as flies up at North Knowesedge....'
'Nowt but mowldy hay 'n' watter aal winter ... eh?....'
'He give us a fiver a head luck....'
'Are y' buyin' the bait then?'
'Toss y' forrit....'

See what I mean ... you might as well be in Afghanistan! Meanwhile the auctioneer is in full flight.... You won't understand him either, so just keep your hands in your pockets and your head down, or y' might end up with a wagon-load of bullin' heifers for your allotment....

'Stand on,' he'll shout ... 'anybody will ... they're a gift ... c'mon where do y' want t' be ... who'll start us at four-fifty ... four hundred then ... bid ...' and off he goes.

It's unlikely you'll actually see anybody bidding. A thumb might move ... an index finger ... an eye-brow raised, a head nod ... a glance, a twitch, they can all mean business....

'You're out over here ...' he says, waving his hammer to everyone on the far side of the ring....

'Bid's on this side mind. No sir, I wouldn't take y' twice' (like hell he wouldn't)....

... The vendor looks dejected ... 'I think he expected a wee bit more for these ... I'll take another fiver ... Are y' all finished then?' Bang! End of chapter....

'… I think it's called a microlight …'

'... Inland Revenue, bank statement, four bills, a final demand, no subsidy cheques ... and you've got a dead lamb in the bottom field ...'

'Jack, it's that bloke who bought the cow.... He says somebody might call in for the luck money t'night ...'

'... who have we today? The man from MLC, two Health and Safety, one Trading Standards, RSPCA, and a dealer from Barnsley.... Could be a moderate trade!'

Incident...

Back in the mart car park there has been an altercation between a simple peasant and a power-crazed inspector from the Trading Standards office.... A small crowd has gathered to monitor the proceedings.

'One of your sheep is quite seriously lame,' says the power-crazed inspector.

'So bloody what?' says the simple peasant. 'All my sheep are lame some of the time ... I could show y' far worse cases than this...!'

'This one cannot be presented for auction,' insists the PCI. 'She is in considerable discomfort....'

'Nonsense, she's just pretendin',' protests the peasant ... 'looking for sympathy....'

'She can barely put one foot past the other,' insists PCI. 'You shouldn't have brought her here ... it is cruel and heartless to expose the poor creature to the stress of the mart....'

'I tell y' there's nowt the matter with 'er' says the peasant ... 'she's a tremendous yow ... reared twins every year since she was a gimmer...!'

'Be that as it may,' insists PCI, 'I am ordering you under rule 211 (sub section f) EEC regulation 27, and the authority vested in me by the Cruelty to Old Yowes Agreement Brussels 1993 to remove this pathetic creature forthwith from the mart premises, and take her home for veterinary treatment.'

'But she'll make a right good price,' says the peasant. 'And nobody'll notice a bit of a limp when she's beltin' round the ring with twenty-nine others....' I'll make sure they're kept on the move ... y' can depend on *that*!'

'The animal is a cripple,' says PCI. 'It's a disgrace ... the RSPCA will have to be informed ... there's nothing more to say ... legal proceedings may follow.'

'Oh, alright,' says the peasant, 'you win.... Let the old bugger out....'

That confrontation took place several hours ago ... and it appears the triumphant official then took it upon himself to personally draw out the poor lame, pathetic, crippled creature, and remove her from the pen. Surprisingly, while he was performing this official task, the old yow knocked him down into the mart clarts, and ran off at astonishing speed. Now, with the sale over and the light fading in the west, she still hadn't been apprehended, in spite of the efforts of mart staff and several wagon drivers.

Meanwhile the Power Crazed Inspector had

long since gone home. Sadly he was quite seriously lame.

'... not much fun being a single parent, is it?'

'... the HILLS are alive with the sound of music ...'

'... are you kidding! *Two* sheep are no bloody good ... one of them'll die for sure!'

'Aye well, that's half of it gone already!'

Him 'n' Her...

Obviously no peasant could survive for long in any modern urban society where sexual equality, social and political correctness are constantly on the agenda. The new 'militant', self-confident, emancipated woman holds few attractions for this weatherbeaten auld chauvinist.

But of course this man has never worked in a crowded mixed office ... groped his way to work on the Piccadilly line ... been stuck in a slow lift with a fast secretary. His has always been a distinctly male world in which women seldom compete ... no threat....

In fact it has never occurred to him that Gladys was anything other than a different species altogether ... on her own peculiar wavelength ... not better or worse, y' understand, ... just different.... Thank God. Certainly there was never any need for her to burn underwear, or chain herself to a muckspreader — and the very idea that the lady might sue some bloke for harassment in the hayshed is quite ludicrous. She'd either be incontrollably chuffed — or she'd belt 'im!

And yet domestic harmony at Clartiehole can often be a somewhat fragile affair. Perhaps the extraordinary pressures of weather, sheep and the Common Agricultural Policy make this inevitable, and in spite of being an 'absolute treasure' most of the time, Sep can occasionally be quite difficult to live with....

Gladys has probably known him since he was a raw youth, and any early suspicions she might've had of old-world rural charm and wit have long since evaporated.... The scruffy, smelly old fool is now either miserable because events are going badly ... or reluctant to smile in case *she* gets the impression things might be going well — and suggests a holiday....

There may be attempts to inject a little culture into his barren artistic life now and then — but it's a futile exercise. As far as Sep's concerned, unless Gilbert and Sullivan are wholesale butchers — he's not really interested. Operatic duets are like family rows at lambin' time — and grown men who ponce about in thermal tights chasing swans over a frozen lake are obviously not to be trusted!

And Sep hates Christmas — that festive fiasco which goes on from September to January, polluted by contrived merriment, sickly advertising ... unnecessary baubles and total household upheaval. All of it renders Sep nigh suicidal.... Each year he threatens to hide away somewhere until it's all over. But of course ... there's no escape. Gladys has invited the kids ... they've bought him a new pair of Y-fronts and another pocket knife. There's a bloody great tree in the sitting room ... and every house is the same ... he's trapped...!

Luckily he still has the livestock to feed ... at least the hemmel provides some kind of refuge — until he's forced to come back inside, half frozen.

The hard working peasant cannot really afford to be unwell. Yet, however brave he may be, this seldom prevents him suspecting he might sometimes have a terminal disorder — as yet a mystery to medical science.

Gladys will occasionally have a slight cold ... but Sep (unluckily) is generally attacked by a particularly virulent strain of oriental flu. Gladys has a headache — with Sep it will probably be a brain tumour. A sprained ankle is almost certainly broken ... indigestion immediately suggests poisoning by Gladys or persons unknown.... At the same time, illness in anyone else is greeted with a dismissive snort ... 'It'll be nowt man ... he was always soft as clarts....'

'... take my word for it, dear ... the big, ugly sod will be extinct long before the mule yow!'

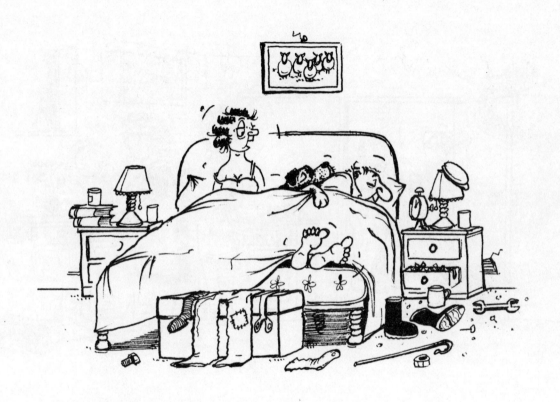

'… I've definitely got a headache comin' on …'

'Where on earth did you find him, Sandra? He's the spittin' image of your Dad!'

'I suppose it must be the moonlight.... But how about helpin' me and Sweep with the lambin'
for the rest of your life?'

'Yes, he's out of danger ... we found a barley awn cross-over in his belly button ...'

'It's still not too late, dear … there's got to be a nice rich solicitor out there somewhere …'

Face to Face...

One breezy Sunday morning in July Mr Bert Townie rose early and, accompanied by the family's poorly bred whippet bitch, set off for a walk along by Primrose wood.

Bert looked forward eagerly to this stroll in the country. After another boring week on the factory floor it was postively therapeutic to feel the wind on his face again, breathe in the smells of grass, trees, corn — and hear the birds, catch a glimpse of a rabbit....

Cilla the whippet was almost euphoric as she scampered and sniffed about in the undergrowth by the side of the path, never wandering too far from her master.

The old narrow track was seldom used these days; in fact Bert couldn't remember ever meeting anybody else on his walks. Maybe not many people knew about it, and this suited Bert well enough.... He was just looking for some peace 'n' quiet, away from work, kids and Acacia Avenue ... a time to talk to himself ... to dream a little.

And then suddenly he realised the path had come to a dead end.

Funny ... he'd always come this way before ... hadn't he? Out past the new trading estate, through the wicket gate behind the electricity sub-station. There was a public footpath sign (almost hidden in the thorn hedge now ... but he was sure it was still there). Perhaps he'd missed a turning somewhere, maybe he should've gone left at the stile half a mile back. Anyway, Bert and Cilla were now staring at a lethal barbed wire fence — and beyond that a sea of yellow corn.

Worse was to come ... emerging from the corn, rising like some prehistoric monster from the deep, there appeared what Bert at first took to be a tramp. That was until he saw the man was brandishing a firearm probably dating back to the Napoleonic wars. He was big, red-faced and obviously upset…. 'Who the hell are you?' he demanded.

'Ah, good morning,' said Bert. 'Lovely morn….'

'Where do y' think *you're* goin'?' growled the peasant.

'Just a little stroll with the dog,' says Mr T.

'Sod off!' snarled Sep.

'Public footpath …' protested Bert. 'There's a signpost back there somewhere….'

'Rubbish,' says Sep. 'This is private land … go on, bugger off back to your crime-infested housing estate!'

He'd moved closer now, just on the other side of his barbed wire defences, and the aged canon seemed to be pointed carelessly at Cilla.

'Wait a minute,' says Bert, becoming a little agitated himself, 'Who do you think *you* are, shoutin' and threatening me? You're just a farmer … I mean you're hardly Lord of the Manor are y'? You're obviously not the Duke of Norfolk or Prince Charles, or … Barbara bleedin' Cartland!' (she was the only other person he could think of at the time — and he regretted it later).

'Listen,' says Sep, waving a finger at the foe, 'this is *my* farm … lived here all m' life … m' father before that … and it's difficult enough makin' ends meet without little townie wasters like yourself wanderin' about with killer dogs!'

'No, *you* listen,' Bert protested. 'You don't realise just how lucky *you* are … you're very privileged … and what's more you're very highly subsidised, by ME!' (he shouted that bit). 'Subsidised to grow crops, rear animals … and come t' think of it even subsidised t' grow

119

nowt!' He was wagging his own finger now. 'Y' live in a mini-mansion surrounded by acres and acres of green fields. Y' don't know you're born ... you wouldn't last five minutes in Acacia Avenue!'

Bert paused there because his brain had slipped temporarily out of gear — and Sep leapt in.

'You're bloody right I wouldn't,' he roared. 'There's no way I'd live where *you* live, that's for sure.... Dirty, noisy place, full o' queers and blacks and drugs and crime everywhere.... It's not safe ... gone t' the dogs.... That's why the likes of you come trespassin' ... in fact most of you would want to come and live here if y' could — in the real world!' (Sep often referred to his world as the real world. He wasn't exactly sure what he meant, but it sounded right.)

'THE REAL WORLD?' Bert exploded ... 'the real world! ... Where the hell is the real world? Certainly not on your private little patch it isn't, where the taxpayer forks out for set-aside and Arable Area payments and ewe quotas...!'

Sep was a little more subdued. 'How do you know all that stuff?' he asked.

'Oh I can read y' know,' says Mr Townie. 'I know all about the Integrated Administrative Control System, and the Countryside Stewardship scheme, and the rest.... And you think *that's* the real world ... you must be joking! I mean what does an arrogant old bugger like you know about dole queues, ethnic violence, noisy neighbours, lawless kids, old ladies mugged in dark alleys and life in a tower block? That world's just as real as yours if you happen to live there y'know ... This *real* world you talk about ... it's every-where mate ... everybody lives in it. Some are just born a bit luckier than others, that's all!'

Sep had been rather taken aback by the man, even felt he might have come second in this confrontation — so he played what he thought was his trump card … 'I bet you're one of those left-wing social workers,' he said with a 'knowing' smile….

'Huh, not really,' said Bert quietly. 'T' tell y' the truth I'm so disillusioned with politics, I might not vote for any of them next time. In fact that might be what this is all about … maybe the politicians are the only ones *NOT* in the real world any more!'

'I'll drink t' that,' said Sep. 'Do y' fancy a quick beer before y' walk back?' He produced a piece of blue baler twine from his trouser pocket. 'Fetch the dog with you,' he said. 'But keep her tied up … m' old yowes don't like strange dogs. On the other hand Sweep's not fussy who he meets, — so y' could end up with a very peculiar litter of pups if you're not careful…!'

'Sorry sir … I'm afraid he's in a meeting all day …'

'He's just a bloody nuisance … costs a fortune every year….
It's high time he made himself useful!'

124

'... actually he's been in a remarkably good mood lately.... Of course it can all change in the twinkling of an eye ...'

'Yes, I think we must assume the last yow has finally lambed now!'

'... well I don't mind telling' y', Peter ... I didn't budget for this!'